I0844395

SCIENCE OF MONEY

Timeless teachings about riches, greed, and happiness.

BY

TOMMY M. MACMILLAN

Introduction

Discover the Science of financial decisions.

How does the stock market work? When is the best time to buy or sell assets? And how much money do you need to save each year if you want to retire at a certain age?

These are the kinds of questions that dominate private financial discussions. However, an important factor is frequently overlooked. This is the human element, or the interaction of actual people with their money. Morgan Housel thinks that understanding financial decision-making necessitates an understanding of this component. You don't need to study interest rates to understand why people go into debt or waste their wealth; instead, you need to delve into the all-too-human history of jealousy, greed, and optimism.

And that is exactly what we shall do in the next volumes.

You'll also learn as you go.

1) 1.how personal experiences shape investment decisions

2) Why buying 99 duds to locate a single Picasso; and

3) How jealousy drives investors to risk everything they own.

CHAPTER 1

PSYCHOLOGY OF MONEY

Money psychology explores at the complex relationship that occurs between our emotions, behavior, and financial decisions. Understanding the psychological aspects of money can assist us in making better financial decisions and developing a more positive relationship with our money. Let us now get into some specifics:

1. Money and Emotions:

Money frequently evokes intense emotions such as joy, worry, dread, or uncertainty. Money's emotional attachment can influence how we view financial risks, make investment decisions, and engage in impulsive spending. Making wise financial decisions necessitates becoming aware of our emotional reactions to money.

2. The Value of Perception:

Perception strongly influences our financial decisions. Our subjective beliefs of wealth, success, and financial well-being can influence how much we spend, save, and live. Understanding how our viewpoint effects our financial behavior enables us to reconsider and realign our priorities with our long-term objectives.

3. Behavior biases:

Cognitive biases exist in humans and can influence our financial decisions. Common biases include loss aversion (the tendency to feel losses more intensely than rewards), confirmation bias (favoring information that supports current thoughts), and herd mentality (following the crowd). Recognizing our biases can help us make more objective financial decisions.

4. Delay in gratification:

Long-term financial success necessitates the ability to delay gratification. It requires resisting the impulse to choose immediate gratification over larger, long-term advantages. This talent improves long-term goal-setting, savings, and investing approaches. Understanding the relationship between short-term costs and long-term benefits is crucial for financial progress.

5. Money and Relationships:

Money can have a significant impact on our relationships. Financial disagreements or variations in money values can affect marriages, relationships, and friendships. Building healthy and successful financial relationships necessitates open and honest communication about personal financial attitudes, goals, and expectations.

6. Financial well-being and happiness:

While money is crucial for meeting our basic needs, research indicates that having more money over a certain income level does not imply enhanced enjoyment. Investing in experiences, relationships, and personal development often has a longer-term impact on our overall happiness than financial items.

7. Financial Literacy and Education:

Improving financial literacy is necessary for making wise financial decisions. Personal finance, budgeting, investing, and risk management education equips us with the knowledge and skills we need to navigate the financial world's complexities.

Understanding the psychology of money may assist us in making better informed financial decisions, overcoming biases and emotional decision-making, and developing a more positive relationship with money. We are constantly on a path of self-reflection, education, and awareness in our financial life.

Please keep in mind that everyone's financial decisions and circumstances are unique. It is best to get professional advice from financial specialists or advisers.

CHAPTER 2

MONEY AND FEELINGS

Money has a strong emotional value and can elicit a wide range of emotions in us. Our financial circumstances, beliefs, and experiences impact our emotional response to money. Take note of the following critical points:

1. Importance Emotional:

Money carries emotional significance because it represents stability, independence, power, and the ability to meet our needs and desires. When we meet financial goals or receive desired products, we may experience positive emotions such as satisfaction, happiness, and pride. Money, on the other hand, can provoke undesirable emotions such as worry, fear, jealously, or guilt, particularly when we are experiencing financial troubles or comparing ourselves to others.

2. Scripts for Hire:

Money scripts are the beliefs and attitudes we develop about money throughout our lives. These scripts are influenced by our upbringing, cultural background, and personal experiences. Our financial scripts have a significant impact on our emotional relationship with money. Someone who believes "money is the root of all evil" may feel guilty or uneasy about amassing wealth, whereas someone who views money as a measure of success may derive a sense of self-worth from their financial position.

3. Emotional Spending:

Emotions may influence our shopping decisions. Emotional spending occurs when we use money to manage or cope with our emotions, such as going shopping when we're sad. Understanding emotional spending triggers and patterns enables us to distinguish between genuine necessities and impulsive, emotionally motivated purchases. Long-term financial stability necessitates the development of healthy coping methods that go beyond material consumption.

4. Anxiety and Financial Stress:

Financial anxiety and stress are significant contributors of anxiety and stress. Debt, job security, and financial obligations can all have a negative impact on our mental and emotional wellbeing. Addressing financial stress necessitates careful planning, seeking financial advice when necessary, and implementing strategies to manage and minimize financial issues.

5. Money and Relationships:

Money can have a significant impact on our relationships. Financial squabbles, clashes over spending habits, or discrepancies in financial objectives can strain relationships, marriages, and family dynamics. Open and honest discussions about money, as well as creating shared financial goals and collaborating on financial decisions, all contribute to good relationships founded on trust and understanding.

6. Financial Security and Happiness:

Though money might bring a sense of security and comfort, studies show that above a certain income level, further wealth does not always translate into greater enjoyment. On the other hand, experiences, relationships, personal progress, and a sense of purpose have a stronger impact on overall life satisfaction and well-being.

Understanding the emotional side of money allows us to have a more positive relationship with it. It requires assessing our financial attitudes and scripts, as well as gaining control over our emotional spending habits. Positive money attitudes and emotional resilience can lead to greater financial well-being and overall life satisfaction.

Please keep in mind that everyone's financial and emotional circumstances are unique. If your emotional relationship with money is affecting your well-being, seeking professional treatment from a financial therapist or counselor may be beneficial.

CHAPTER 3

A DIFFERENT TAKE ON THE ECONOMY AND MONEY.

The story of the Great Depression is well-known. Following a disastrous stock market crash in 1929, the global economy began a decade of slow deterioration.

In the United States, the "roaring twenties" came to an end. Businesses faltered, families were forced to sell their farms and homes, and hard-earned money vanished. Poverty and unemployment soared, but hope for a better tomorrow declined. This version of events is now widely accepted. That makes logical; after all, it describes millions of Americans' experiences. It does, however, leave something critical out of the picture.

The central theme of this chapter is that everyone has an opinion about the economy and money. When John F. Kennedy ran for president in 1960, he was asked about his experiences during the Great Depression. Many voters were surprised by his reaction.

He said the Kennedys were already wealthy in 1929. And their wealth did not diminish over the next ten years; rather, it expanded. By 1939, the family had more employees and a larger home than at the start of the decade. He had no idea how hard many of his fellow citizens had endured until he arrived at Harvard and began studying the Depression.

It was discovered that not all Americans were in the same condition. That was one of the ways Kennedy persuaded Americans that he was more than an out-of-touch elite, but a legitimate president. But it is not only the wealthy and the poor who have varied economic experiences; we all do.

The son of an unemployed farmhand and the son of a well-known Manhattan stockbroker not only come from different origins, but they also learn about money in very different ways, such as risk and return. However, as we will see later, the same holds true for similarly well-off people based on their unique life experiences.

A wealthy individual who grew up during periods of enormous inflation, for example, will have a different financial viewpoint than a similarly wealthy someone who has only ever known stable prices. The lessons learnt from these many perspectives have an impact on what we do with money.

We all want to believe we understand how the world works, but in reality, we only get a sliver of the truth. And the first thing to remember about money psychology is that we know far less than we would want to believe.

CHAPTER 4

PERSONAL EXPERIENCE HAS AN IMPACT ON FINANCIAL DECISIONS.

When economists simulate financial behavior, they usually rely on a convenient fiction: rational persons making self-interested decisions in order to maximize their benefits.

Of course, reality is a little more complicated than this great idea. Take, for example, the lottery. The average low-income household in the United States spends $411 on lottery tickets each year. At the same time, more than 40% of all households find it difficult to come up with $400 in an emergency. This 40% consists of the same low-income families who spend little more than $400 on lottery tickets.

Is this appropriate behavior? Hardly. However, it is not unreasonable. If you live paycheck to paycheck, you are unlikely to have enough money for needs, as well as many alone pleasures such as trips. Playing the lottery is a long shot, but it's better than having no possibility of acquiring the high-quality things that the wealthy take for granted.

This chapter's major premise is that personal experience influences financial decisions. Irrational phone calls are more common than you might think. Consider Ulrike

Malmendier and Stefan Nagel's 2006 study. They combed through data from the Survey of Consumer Finances, a long-running research project that examines how Americans spend their money. Malmendier and Nagel wanted to determine what factors influence people's investment decisions.

Their reaction? The state of the economy when the investors were teenagers. In other words, our risk tolerance is shaped by our history. This isn't the kind of logic found in economics textbooks, but it's intuitively evident, like buying lottery tickets. If an investor's late teens and early twenties were marked by high inflation, he or she was far less likely to invest in bonds later in life. If inflation remained low during these formative years, investors were content to keep their money in bonds as they aged, regardless of whether inflation rose along the way.

Stocks take a similar path. Investors continued to invest in the stock market if it was performing well in early adulthood; if it was underperforming at the same age, they avoided it. Assume your birth year is 1970. Between your mid-teens and early twenties, the Sample 500 increased threefold. Anyone who bought stock in the companies mentioned on that stock made a fortune. People born in 1950 had a different perspective on the market, which was mostly dormant at the time. Importantly, investment decisions did not change even when the market did, implying that real-world facts did not influence gut decisions made early in life.

CHAPTER 5

OUR CURRENT ECONOMIC CONCEPTS ARE STILL IN THEIR INFANCY.

A toy poodle bears no resemblance to its wild ancestors, which were not dissimilar to wolves. This should come as no surprise given the ten-thousand-year history of domestication of today's dog breeds. Even so, dog owners are occasionally astounded by their dogs' natural, murderous reactions when they see a squirrel or a cat. It turns out that ten millennia haven't removed these deeply ingrained wild characteristics.

But what does dog domestication have to do with monetary psychology? A great deal. The main point of this chapter is that our current economic concepts are still in their infancy. Why are so many of us such slackers when it comes to money?

One explanation is that it is new in the grand scheme of things. The first coins were struck in 600 BC by King Alyattes of Lydia in an Iron-Age kingdoms in modern-day Turkey. Furthermore, it pales in comparison to more complex economic principles. Take into account retirement. Prior to WWII, most Americans worked until they died. Despite the fact that life expectancy was lower back then, half of all males over the age of 65 were still working in the 1940s. The introduction of Social Security after World War II began to change things, but retirement remained an unattainable goal for most American workers until the 1980s, when the average monthly Social Security payment surpassed $1,000, adjusted for inflation. Only a wealthy few could previously afford to retire in their mid-sixties. That means that one of the most basic economic principles we use today is less than two generations old. The 401(k), the primary method of funding retirement, did not even exist until 1978, and the Roth IRA retirement plan did not even exist until 1998!

Other crucial ideas and behaviors aren't much older. Hedge funds were only introduced a quarter-century ago, whereas index funds are only 50 years old. Even consumer debt, which is now one of the most important drivers of economic development in the United States, became widespread only after the GI Bill made it easier for ordinary Americans to borrow money in 1944.

If we're bad at financial planning and decision-making, we're not insane; we're just inexperienced!

CHAPTER 6

LUCK HAS A GREATER INFLUENCE ON FINANCIAL SUCCESS THAN YOU MIGHT THINK.

A few years ago, the author asked Nobel Laureate economist Robert Schiller what he'd like to know about investing that isn't well-known. Schiller's answer: "exact role of luck in successful outcomes. "Luck is a difficult concept to grasp. Few investors and entrepreneurs would deny that it plays a role in theory, but quantifying the extent to which it is responsible for one business's success - or failure - is difficult. We also believe it is impolite to attribute other people's success to chance. As a result, we frequently undervalue the role of chance in financial decision-making. That is a mistake. The key point is that luck plays a larger role in financial success than you might think.

Income of two siblings correlates more closely than height or weight, according to economist Bhashkar Mazumder. To put it another way, if your brother is wealthy and tall, chances are you are wealthy rather than tall. This association is simple to understand. Siblings from the same family are likely to benefit from the same opportunities. When parents send one of their children to a reputable school, they frequently send his brother as well. Identify a pair of wealthy brothers, however, and you'll find two people who do not believe Mazumder's study applies to their family.

This is due to the nature of human psychology. We frequently undervalue or exaggerate the role of chance in outcome. If we succeed, it is due to our hard work; if we fail, it is due to bad luck. When others fail, we aren't nearly as forgiving. In many circumstances, we blame failure on character faults such as sloth or shortsightedness rather than poor luck.

Unfortunately, our success-obsessed culture isn't much assistance here. Forbes does not honor outstanding investors who went bankrupt because they were unfortunate and the market crashed. It does, however, glorify second-rate or foolish speculators who struck gold.

That puts us in a bind. When it comes to money, we need to know not just what works and what doesn't, but also how to include unpredictability into our models. We may not be able to accomplish Schiller's ambition of accounting for the "exact role" of chance, but as we'll see, we can control it.

CHAPTER 7

CONCENTRATING ON GENERAL TRENDS RATHER THAN INDIVIDUAL EXAMPLES MIGHT ASSIST YOU IN MAKING BETTER DECISIONS.

Bill Gates once said, *"Success is a terrible teacher."*

According to Gates, success mislead smart people into dismissing the importance of luck, which leads them to believe they can't lose. That, paradoxically, is a good method to ensure that you will lose.

The main takeaway from this chapter is that focusing on general trends rather than individual examples will help you make better decisions.

So, how should you include chance and luck in your financial decisions? What you should not do is fixate on particular examples of individuals. When we analyze extremely successful people, we tend to focus on outliers - billionaires who have revolutionized the way the world works - and this might lead us astray. The main takeaway from this chapter is that focusing on general trends rather than individual examples will help you make better decisions.

Consider John D. Rockefeller, one of the most successful businessmen in history. He ran into a snag when he began to establish his petroleum firm.

The laws of the United States did not allow him to accomplish what he desired. His approach was straightforward: ignore them. His contempt for legal standards was so severe that one court described his company as acting "no better than a common thief."

The success of Rockefeller influences how we conceive about this conduct. Looking back, it's easy to praise his vision and claim that he refused to allow antiquated laws to stifle progress. But what if he had failed? Would we still believe that Rockefeller's example is one to emulate? Most likely not. At most, we'd see him as a failed criminal who showed us what not to do. But, when it comes down to it, the only difference between these two results is chance. A few different rulings here and there, or a shift in the political atmosphere, may have changed Rockefeller's fortunes. More significantly, good fortune is nearly hard to replicate. Even if you replicate every professional move of someone like Warren Buffett, you can't guarantee the dice will fall the same way for you. So here's another option: continue examining patterns of success and failure. The more prevalent a pattern, the more probable it is to apply to your life and financial decisions. For example, research after study reveals that people who have control over the organization of their days are happy with their jobs than those who don't. In contrast to the few occurrences of larger-than-life outliers, it is a wide insight into how you may act right now.

CHAPTER 8

ENVY MIGHT CAUSE YOU TO BE CARELESS.

Capitalism excels at two things: creating riches and creating jealousy.

Consider a rookie baseball player earning $500,000 per year. He's wealthy by any realistic criterion. But if he's in the same club as a superstar like Mike Trout, who gets $36 million a year, he'll be unhappy with his salary. He wants what others possess.

Meanwhile, high-earning individuals like Trout compare themselves to people who make much more. To make the list of America's top 10 highest-paid hedge fund managers in

2018, you needed to earn at least $340 million that year. By that metric, even Trout is a little fry. Envy has no moral ramifications in a commercial society. However, there is a practical issue. The main point of this chapter is that envy may lead to irresponsible behavior. Envy has no moral ramifications in a commercial society. However, there is a practical issue. The main point of this book is that envy may lead to irresponsible behavior.

When does enough become enough? Simply ask Rajat Gupta. Gupta rose through the ranks of management consulting company McKinsey after being born in a slum in Kolkata, India.

He was worth $100 million when he retired in 2007.

He can accomplish anything. Gupta, on the other hand, was jealous. He aspired to become a billionaire.

Gupta, a member of Goldman Sachs' board of directors, learned in 2008 that Warren Buffett was preparing to spend $5 billion to keep the business solvent amid the financial crisis. Sixteen seconds after hearing the news on a conference call, Gupta phoned the number of a hedge fund manager and purchased 175,000 shares of Goldman Sachs.

This was insider trading, which was prohibited. Gupta didn't mind because he'd just made a million dollars. By the time authorities caught up with him, he'd amassed $17 million in a series of shady transactions. It hadn't made him a billionaire, but it had earned him a lengthy prison sentence.

What is the moral of this story? Envy causes unwise decisions, and the cost of those decisions is often larger than the potential advantages. Consider this: If you have an insatiable hunger, you will eat until you are sick. But vomiting up is far worse than any meal, so you don't do it. Leaving possibilities on the table doesn't always mean you're losing out; it's frequently an understanding that attempting to consume everything would lead to regret. To put it another way, don't be Rajat Gupta!

CHAPTER 9

GETTING A FORTUNE IS SIMPLER THAN PRESERVING IT.

Jesse Livermore was one of the best stock market traders in early twentieth-century America. He was born in 1877 and helped to create Wall Street. He was worth $100 million in today's value by the age of 30.

Just before the 1929 stock market crash, Livermore made the finest choice of his career: he went short and gambled that equities would fall. The market, indeed, lost one-third of its overall worth. While fortunes were being liquidated and rumors of insolvent investors leaping from office windows circulated, Livermore came home to his family with good news. He'd just made $3 billion in today's money. Everlasting happiness? Not exactly.

The main point of this chapter is that amassing a fortune is simpler than preserving it. Remember what we said about being a successful bad teacher? Livermore felt he was invincible following his great triumph in 1929. He risked bigger and bigger wagers and lost big time after time until his riches were gone. He committed suicide at a Manhattan club in 1940, destitute and in debt.

It turns out that being rich is sometimes a lot easier than remaining affluent. It's simple to see why those who excel at one typically struggle with the other. Making money is all about taking risks, being optimistic, and being brave. Keeping money is a very other psychological game. It's about the dread of losing all you've worked for. Being affluent also means keeping modest. After 1929, Livermore believed he was a genius who could never make a mistake. He'd be better off admitting that chance had played a factor in his achievement and that it couldn't be repeated continually.

There are many Livermore's out there, but their narratives aren't necessarily as heartbreaking. Approximately 40% of all publicly traded corporations lose their full worth over time. In addition, the Forbes 400 list of America's wealthiest people varies by 20% every decade, excepting cases of death and intra-family transfers.

So, how do you keep what you have? In a nutshell, persistence. The most successful entrepreneurs live for a long period without going bankrupt. They all have one thing in common: they are afraid. When you're frightened of losing, as multibillionaire venture investor Michael Moritz puts it, you look at probable successes through a new lens. Few rewards are large enough to offset the danger of losing everything you own. And when you take that approach, you're a lot more likely to make sensible decisions.

CHAPTER 10

YOU MAY BE INACCURATE 50% OF THE TIME AND YET MAKE A FORTUNE.

Heinz Berggruen, according to his perspective, did not show much potential in his adolescence. He had no notion what to do with his life when he was forced to escape Nazi Germany in 1936.

He worked as a journalist with a sideline in art criticism after studying literature at the University of California, Berkeley. For $100, he purchased a little watercolor by Paul Klee in 1940. It was the start of a lifetime fascination in modern art.

By the 1990s, Berggruen had established himself as one of the most successful art collectors of all time. He sold his collection to the German government for 100 million euros in 2000. Given the quantity of Picassos, Klees, Matisses, and Braques in the collection, that sum was nowhere near its full value, which was expected to reach $1 billion. It was one of the world's most important collections. The basic thesis of this chapter is that you may be wrong half of the time and nevertheless make a fortune.

How did Berggruen gather such an incredible collection of twentieth-century artists? Was it talent or chance? Horizon Research, an investing organization, presents a more intriguing response.

According to the company's survey, all great collectors do the same thing: they purchase vast amounts of art. Some purchases turn out to be wonderful investments, especially if the collector maintains them for a long period. The vast majority, though, are flops. As Horizon's research points out, the objective is to conserve the former until the portfolio return - the entire worth of the collection - "converges upon the return of the best elements in the portfolio."

Berggruen's collection was analogous to an index fund in that his risks were fairly divided among a varied variety of investments. Rather than buying simply products he loved or appreciated, he bought everything he could get his hands on and waited for a few winners to emerge.

This strategy is true for all investments. The long tail is the propensity of a few occurrences to account for the majority of outcomes. This theory is based on a lot of tough math, but when you break it down to the foundations, it's fairly easy. In other words, if you get a few things correctly, you can afford to get more things wrong. Failure is unavoidable; what is essential is the character of your wins. To put it another way, if you own one Picasso, you don't have to worry about the other 99.

FINAL THOUGHTS

These books' major point is:

Financial decision-making in the real world is much more difficult than in economics textbooks. Many decisions, such as buying lottery tickets while you're broke, are illogical, but they make sense in their own way. The same is true for investing decisions, which are usually influenced by people's formative economic experiences in their early adulthood rather than dispassionate appraisals of current market conditions. Simply put, financial decisions are inextricably linked to psychological factors. So, what's the best plan of action? Accept that luck plays a role in success, and learn to fear losing what you have